curious about

SNAKES

BY ALISSA THIELGES

AMICUS

What are you

curious about?

CHAPTER **3** THREE

Snake Behavior

PAGE
16

Curious About is published by Amicus
P.O. Box 227
Mankato, MN 56002
www.amicuspublishing.us

Editor: Rebecca Glaser
Series Designer: Kathleen Petelinsek
Book Designer: Aubrey Harper
Photo Researchers: Alissa Thielges and Omay Ayres

Library of Congress Cataloging-in-Publication Data
Names: Thielges, Alissa, 1995– author.
Title: Curious about snakes / by Alissa Thielges.
Description: Mankato, Minnesota : Amicus, [2023] |
Series: Curious about pets | Audience: Ages 6–9 |
Audience: Grades 2–3 | Summary: "Nine questions that
kids would ask and well-researched, easy-to-understand
answers teach readers about life with a snake, including
pet care and handling techniques. Simple infographics
support visual learning. A Stay Curious! feature encourages
kids to keep asking questions and models media
literacy skills. Includes table of contents, glossary,
and index."—Provided by publisher. Identifiers: LCCN
2021061092 (print) | LCCN 2021061093 (ebook) |
ISBN 9781645493105 (hardcover) |
ISBN 9781681528342 (paperback) |
ISBN 9781645493983 (ebook)
Subjects: LCSH: Snakes as pets–Juvenile literature.
Classification: LCC SF459.S5 T45 2023
(print) | LCC SF459.S5 (ebook) |
DDC 639.3/96–dc23/eng/20220119
LC record available at https://lccn.loc.gov/2021061092
LC ebook record available at https://lccn.loc.gov/2021061093

Photo credits: Dreamstime/Anthonyata 19, Belizar 2,
12–13, Valmedia Creatives 8; iStock/GlobalP 7, Mark
Kostich 6, Natalie Ruffing 16–17, PetlinDmitry cover, 1;
Shutterstock/Egoreichenkov Evgenii 10–11, Eric Isselee
7, 18, Ery Azmeer 3, 20–21, fivespots 7, Fotokon 15,
KAMONRAT 2, 4–5, PetlinDmitry 15, Malpolon 9

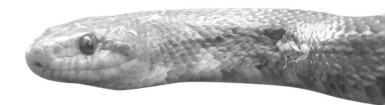

CHAPTER ONE

Are pet snakes dangerous?

No. Pet snakes don't get as big as some wild ones. Their fangs are often smaller, too. They don't have **venom**. Snakes are reptiles. They aren't cuddly pets, but they can be fun to watch. Give them a warm spot and they will bask for hours.

Corn snakes are gentle.
They are popular first reptile pets.

How big will my snake get?

An albino snake has light-colored skin.

It depends on the snake. Green anacondas can get 30 feet (9 m) long! But most pet snakes are about 5 feet (1.5 m). Snakes shed their skin as they grow. It can take 5 years to reach full length. A healthy snake may live 20 years.

KINGSNAKE
UP TO 6 FEET (1.8 M)

MILK SNAKE
ABOUT 3 FEET (0.9 M)

CORN SNAKE
UP TO 6 FEET (1.8 M)

BALL PYTHON
ABOUT 5 FEET (1.5 M)

RED TAIL BOA
ABOUT 10 FEET (3 M)

How often will my snake shed its skin?

A snake grows new skin before shedding its old skin.

About four to eight times a year. This is called **molting**. A snake molts headfirst. It rubs against something rough. Little by little, the skin comes off in one piece. It is inside out. You can see where the scales and eyes were.

DID YOU KNOW?
Before a molt, a snake's eyes are blue and cloudy.

Where do you keep a snake?

**DID
YOU KNOW?**
Snakes love to hide.
Add a box or flowerpot to
a snake's tank.

In a **terrarium**. It is a tank with no water and places to hide. Some snakes like to dig in sand. Others like to crawl on plants. Snakes are **cold-blooded**. They need a heat lamp to stay warm.

A python needs a large tank with a heat lamp.

What do snakes eat?

A snake will swallow
a mouse whole.

Snakes are **carnivores**. They eat other animals. Most are fed frozen mice or rats. Some eat eggs, fish, or insects. Snakes don't eat often. They can be fed once a week. They swallow their food whole and **digest** it slowly.

DID YOU KNOW?
Unlike humans, snakes' jaws aren't **fused** together. They can stretch apart. That's how their mouths open so big!

How do I pick up a snake?

With one hand, grab the middle of the body. Be gentle. Support the snake with your other hand as you lift. Hold it loosely. It may wrap around your arm. This is okay. When the snake wiggles, it wants to be put back down.

Always support a snake with both hands.

CAN I HOLD MY SNAKE HERE?

The Head: No

The Tail: No

The Body: Yes

15

My snake bit me when I pet it. Why?

You may have startled it. Or it may be hungry. To avoid bites, approach a snake slowly. Tap its body gently. Use something other than your hand. If the snake's head is up and it is staring at you, it is in a strike position. Be careful. Wait until it relaxes before picking it up.

A red tail boa does not like to be held.

California kingsnake

Why does my snake flick its tongue?

It is "tasting" the air. Flick, flick. The tips of the tongue pick up smells. Inside the mouth, there are two openings on the roof. This is the **Jacobson's organ**. The tips bring the smells there. Then the brain figures out the scent. Is there danger? Or is it mealtime?

A snake's forked tongue
helps it sense smells.

Do snakes ever blink?

A snake cannot close its eyes.

No. They do not have eyelids. Instead, a clear scale covers each eye. It is called a **spectacle**. It protects the eye. A snake sleeps with its eyes open. How can you tell it's sleeping? It is very still. It may hide to feel safe. Snakes sleep about 16 hours a day!

STAY CURIOUS!

ASK MORE QUESTIONS

Do snakes have ears?

How do snakes move?

Try a BIG QUESTION: Why are some people afraid of snakes?

SEARCH FOR ANSWERS

Search the library catalog or the Internet.
A librarian, teacher, or parent can help you.

Using Keywords
Find the looking glass.

🔍

Keywords are the most important words in your question.

?

If you want to know about:

- whether or not a snake has ears, type: SNAKE EARS
- how a snake moves its body, type: SNAKE MOVEMENT

FIND GOOD SOURCES

Here are some good, safe sources you can use in your research.
Your librarian can help you find more.

Books
Snakes
by Amy McDonald, 2021.

Snakes
by Julie K. Lundgren, 2022.

Internet Sites
The Secret Design and Movement of Slithering Snakes
https://thekidshouldseethis.com/post/38218729229
The Kids Should See This collects videos for kids. This video from the National Science Foundation shows how snakes move.

Understanding Snake Hearing
https://www.thesprucepets.com/are-snakes-bothered-by-loud-noises-1239469
The Spruce Pets is reviewed by veterinarians. The articles teach about pet care.

Every effort has been made to ensure that these websites are appropriate for children. However, because of the nature of the Internet, it is impossible to guarantee that these sites will remain active indefinitely or that their contents will not be altered.

SHARE AND TAKE ACTION

Go to a pet store.
Some have snakes or lizards for sale.

Talk to a vet.
You can ask them questions about any pet snakes they treat.

Visit wild snakes at a zoo.
There are sometimes programs where you can touch or hold a snake.

GLOSSARY

carnivore An animal that eats only meat.

cold-blooded To have a body temperature that changes.

digest To break down food in the organs to make energy for the body.

fused To be firmly attached to something.

Jacobson's organ An organ that helps snakes smell by sensing substances in the air.

molt To lose a covering of hair, feathers, or skin so a new covering can grow.

spectacle A clear scale over a snake's eye that protects the eye from dirt and keeps it moist.

terrarium A clear box used to keep small animals indoors.

venom Poison produced by an animal and used to kill or injure through biting.

INDEX

About the Author

Alissa Thielges is a writer and editor in southern Minnesota who hopes to inspire kids to stay curious about their interests. She doesn't own any pets but would love to have a turtle and dog someday.

24